Japanese
Flowers
in Appliqué

Japanese Flowers in Appliqué

EILEEN CAMPBELL

SALLYMILNER
PUBLISHING

First published in 2010 by
Sally Milner Publishing Pty Ltd
734 Woodville Road
Binda NSW 2583 AUSTRALIA

© Eileen Campbell 2010

Design: Anna Warren, Warren Ventures Pty Ltd
Editing: Vicky Fisher
Photography: Tim Connolly

Printed in China

National Library of Australia Cataloguing-in-Publication data:

Author:	Campbell, Eileen.
Title:	Japanese flowers in applique / Eileen Campbell.
ISBN:	9781863514118 (pbk)
Series:	Milner craft series.
Subjects:	Applique–Japan–Exhibitions.
	Applique–Korea–Exhibitions.
	Quilting–Japan–Exhibitions.
	Quilting–Korea–Exhibitions.
Other Authors/Contributors:	
	Japanese Imagery in Contemporary Quilts (2004 : Japan)
	Japanese Imagery in Contemporary Quilts (2005 : Korea)
Dewey Number:	746.445074

Disclaimer
Information and instructions given in this book are presented in good faith, but no warranty is given nor results
guaranteed, nor is freedom from any patent to be inferred. As we have no control over physical conditions
surrounding application of information herein contained in this book, the author and publisher disclaim any liability
for untoward results.

10 9 8 7 6 5 4 3 2 1

DEDICATION

For my sister Elise Burkitt
Who shares my love of flowers

ACKNOWLEDGEMENTS

Thank you to Libby Renney from Sally Milner Publishing for her serene confidence that a book would eventually happen. It gave me the inspiration to persevere.

Thank you also to Karen Fail who first had the vision of seeing the patterns for this quilt in print.

And, as always, my biggest thanks to my partner Ernie for his constant support in all my quilt-making and writing endeavours.

Contents

Introduction

This quilt was made in response to an invitation from the directors of Kokusai Art and Nihon Vogue of Tokyo to submit a quilt for an exhibition entitled Japanese Imagery in Contemporary Quilts. The exhibition included one quilt by each of 75 Japanese and 25 Western quilt artists.

The exhibition opened in Tokyo on 28 December 2004 in the Nihonbashi Mitsukoshi Department Store. It then travelled to venues in Hiroshima, Fukuoka, Kagoshima, Sapporo, Kyoto and Takamatsu. Altogether, the exhibition attracted over 105,000 visitors in Japan. In October 2005 the exhibition travelled to Korea where it was shown in the Chojun Textile and Quilt Museum, and Sookmyung Women's University Museum in Seoul.

I have travelled to Japan at various times in Summer, Autumn and Spring. The flowers in many temple and public gardens make a stunning display, and I especially loved the Meiji Jingu Iris Garden. These flowers were the inspiration for my quilt. The brilliant colours of the Japanese maples in Autumn overshadowed the softer tones of some of the Summer and Spring flowers so the maple leaves are quilted in gold around the border.

The Quilt

FABRICS

Some background information is necessary before you decide on fabrics and the overall design of your quilt.

Many of the fabrics used in this quilt are silk. The shaded and black backgrounds are Japanese kimono silk. The plain grey of the background blocks is Thai silk. The flowers are also Thai silk. Silk is wonderful to work with and gives the finished quilt a very rich look. The only problem is that it can fray easily. This does not matter for appliqués if you are using the fusible web method, as the webbing holds the edges firm until they are stitched. If you use silk for the background fabric then it is best to cut the blocks a little larger than you need and zigzag over the edges to stop the silk fraying as you work.

If you prefer to work with cotton rather than silk there are some beautifully shaded cotton fabrics available that would give a similar effect as the original quilt. Hand-dyed cottons would also be an excellent choice. Hand-dyed, plain or softly patterned fabrics would be very suitable for the flowers.

The Blocks Layout diagrams and sizes of the blocks are given in both metric and imperial measurements. Use one or the other or else the quilt top will not fit together.

The layout diagrams have been altered slightly from the original quilt so that the sashings width is consistent, with the exception of the block on the lower right-hand side where there needs to be space for the iris in the border. This is because when I made this quilt I used some odd-sized pieces of silk for the blocks which meant that they did not fit together exactly. Adjustments then had to be made to the sashing.

In most cases, the changes to the block sizes are small. However, the two blocks on the lower right-hand side are now 7.5 cm (3 in) wider. Add more flowers to the designs for these blocks to fill the spaces.

Requirements

For blocks	1.75 m (2 yd)
Sashing	1.75 m (2 yd)
Borders, block edgings and binding	1.75 m (2 yd)
Backing fabric	3.2 m (3¾ yd)
For 3D Broderie Perse butterflies — printed fabric that can be cut for approximately 10 whole butterflies	
Or to make your own 3D butterflies	25 cm (¼ yd)
Batting	1.6 m X 1.6 m (65 in X 65 in)
Braid or heavy gold thread	40 m (42 yd)
Iron-on stabiliser	1.75m (2 yd)
Vliesofix or other double-sided fusible paper	1 m (1 yd)
Medium-weight iron-on Vilene for 3D butterflies	25 cm (¼ yd)

APPLIQUÉS

Greens — At least three different greens can be used for leaves:

Light green for waterlily, hydrangea and rose	25 cm (¼ yd)
Mid-green for chrysanthemum	10 cm (4 in)
Dark green for iris, camellia and peony	50 cm (½ yd)
Shades of purple/mauve/blue for iris	50 cm (½ yd)
White for rose, some peonies, waterlily, camellias, chrysanthemums and blossoms	30 cm ($^1/_3$ yd)
Autumn tones for chrysanthemums	25 cm (¼ yd)
Red for camellia, waterlily and peonies	25 cm (¼ yd)
Pink for waterlily, rose, blossom and peonies	25 cm (¼ yd)

THREADS

Machine embroidery rayons to match appliqués
Bobbinfil, 'The Bottom Line' or polyester thread for the bobbin
Monofilament thread or your favourite quilting thread to stipple
    quilt the blocks
Monofilament thread to attach the butterflies
Gold thread for quilted leaves in the border
Polyester thread to match backing for quilting

SEWING MACHINE

¼ in foot for piecing
Zigzag or open-toed embroidery foot for satin stitching
Darning foot
Walking foot (if your machine does not have dual feed)
Braiding foot
Size 75 or 80 machine needles
Size 75 or 80 Metalfil or Topstitch needle for gold thread

MISCELLANEOUS

Tracing paper for appliqué designs
Stitch n' Tear or greaseproof paper for tracing the quilted leaves
HB or H pencil
Approximately 500 2.5 cm (1 in) safety pins to baste the quilt together
Tapestry needle
Masking tape
Small sharp scissors
Appliqué mat
Silicone paper (baking paper)
Tweezers

The Sewing Machine

KEEPING YOUR MACHINE CLEAN

Always make sure that your machine is totally free of lint around the bobbin case. Clean it thoroughly before using it and after every few bobbins, especially when sewing through all the layers of Vliesofix and backings. Keep the machine oiled according to the manufacturer's instructions.

MACHINE FEET

Use an appliqué or clear plastic foot for satin-stitching. An open-toed embroidery foot is excellent as you can see your stitching clearly.

For attaching braid, a braiding foot, or for wider braids an open-toed embroidery foot will help guide the braid through.

Use a darning foot for embroidery, outline quilting or free-motion quilting (Cornelli work or stipple quilting).

A walking foot is invaluable for quilting straight or gently curved lines. A walking foot feeds the layers of fabric evenly through the machine, eliminating bubbles on either side of the quilt sandwich. Some machines have an even-feed foot built into the machine instead of a walking foot. If your machine has this, it should be engaged for straight-line quilting.

If your machine has a control for adjusting the pressure on the presser foot, then decrease the pressure a little for satin-stitching as it allows you more freedom of movement with your fabric.

NEEDLES

The needle should be sharp and the correct size for the thread and fabric — a size 80 needle is good for most work. Change the needle after every six to eight hours of stitching, or more often if it becomes blunt.

For appliqué and machine embroidery it is best to use a Metalfil needle size 75 or 80. This needle has a bigger eye and helps to stop the thread from breaking. It is especially good for metallic threads when appliquéing or quilting.

However, if you are satin-stitching or embroidering on silks or fine fabrics then use a size 70 needle as it does not leave big holes. Match the needle and thread to the fabrics you are using.

When machine-quilting using some of the thicker decorative threads, a size 90 needle may be required to stitch through the multiple layers.

THREADS

For satin-stitching and free-machine embroidery the best results are achieved by using machine embroidery rayon threads, especially for satin-stitching. These will give you a smooth even look with a lovely sheen that you cannot obtain by using cotton threads, although these can also be used depending on the effect that you want. There are many brands to choose from.

A number 40 rayon thread is excellent and is the size most widely available. For more defined stitching, number 30 embroidery rayon can be used, for example stitching the flower stamens.

A wide range of shiny metallic threads is available. The easiest ones to use have a smooth finish. These are excellent for highlights and special effects.

In the bobbin use Bobbinfil or a fine polyester or polycotton thread when appliquéing directly onto the background. 'The Bottom Line' (a Superior Threads fine polyester) is designed for using in the bobbin or for fine appliqué and comes in a large range of colours. Bobbinfil comes in black or white.

If your tension is set correctly, you should be able to use white with light-coloured top thread, and black with dark top thread and not have it show on the top. Being very fine (number 70), the Bobbinfil or 'The Bottom Line' helps to give a smooth, even, satin-stitch with the rayon top threads. If you have trouble with the bobbin thread showing on the top of your work, one solution is to use the same colour thread in both the bobbin and through the needle.

For three-dimensional appliqués, it is best to use the same thread through the needle and in the bobbin, as the colour will then be even on all visible edges. When using rayon thread in the bobbin, wind the bobbin a little more slowly than usual so you do not stretch or break the thread.

Japanese Flowers in Appliqué

Satin-stitching

Check your machine manual for the recommendations for satin-stitching. The top thread tension will usually have to be adjusted to produce a smooth, even satin-stitch without any bobbin thread showing.

To do this, loosen the top tension a little. For example, if the normal setting is 4, then reduce it to 3. If your machine has + or - on the tension dial, then move it toward the minus sign. You may find that you need to reduce the tension even more than this. Stitch a test piece, using stabilised fabric with contrasting threads in the top and the bobbin. Take it out of the machine and look at the back. Your aim is to have the satin-stitching pull underneath slightly, so that the top thread is seen on either side of the bobbin thread. There will probably be more top colour showing along one side than the other. If the top thread is not being pulled through enough, lower the top tension a little more and try again. Keep this test piece and write your settings on it so that you have it as a reference. On some machines, threading the bobbin thread through the special hole for buttonholes has the same effect as loosening the top tension. You may or may not have to adjust the top tension a little more.

What you are trying to achieve are zigzag stitches that are close enough together to appear as a solid line but not so close that the stitches bunch up and jam the machine. There should be enough length so that if you let go of the fabric the feed-dogs will push the fabric through the machine without any problem. This will vary from one machine to another. Again, check the instructions in the machine manual for the recommended setting, but be prepared to adjust further to get the stitch you require.

The complex mixture of fabrics in a project can affect your machine settings, so practise sewing on a sample of the fused layers of fabrics and stabiliser used in each particular project. This will allow you to test tension, stitches and thread colour.

For most appliqués the satin-stitch width is between 1.5 mm and 2 mm (up to $^1/_{16}$ in). If you have larger appliqués, a larger stitch can be used. At less than 1 mm ($^1/_{32}$ in), the satin-stitch becomes too narrow to hold the appliqué in place. For something very small, it is better to use free-machining. Your stitches should rest mostly on the appliqué piece, coming over only slightly onto the background fabric.

Begin and end the stitching with a few fastening straight stitches on one spot. Lift the presser foot and move your work very slightly forward so that the first zigzags cover the starting point. When finishing off, lift the presser foot and put the fastening stitches just behind the last couple of stitches or stitch in one spot right beside the zigzags on the appliqué side. Alternatively, pull the top thread through and tie it off at the back. Do not stitch forward and back over the satin-stitch as this will create a lump.

The aim is to sew at right angles to the edge of the appliqué piece you are stitching. If you need to change the angle to go around a curve, stop with the needle in the wide part of the curve, lift the presser foot, turn your work slightly and do a few more stitches. Repeat this pivoting step as many times as you find it necessary to complete stitching the curve smoothly. For a concave curve you will be stopping with the needle on the appliqué, and for a convex curve, on the background fabric. With experience, you will find that you can control your stitching at a fair speed, turning the work as you go. This will eliminate some of the starting and stopping.

Using a 1.5 mm to 2 mm (up to $^1/_{16}$ in) stitch, it is not necessary to taper points on leaves etc. Instead, continue to the top of the point. Leave the needle down and turn your work. Raise the needle and reposition the work so that your first stitching in the other direction covers the previous couple of stitches. This will give you a blunt point and is very easy to do without affecting the good appearance of the motif.

It may not matter if your stitching goes a little off line and moves too far onto the appliqué; for example, if it is a leaf or flower and the basic shape is not altered appreciably. If this is the case, lift the excess fabric with your fingernail, then use a pair of very sharp scissors to trim off the piece. If trimming the appliqué will spoil the shape, or if you have stitched too far off the appliqué and it is no longer held in place, then you must take the stitching out and re-stitch it. The easiest way to do this is to turn your work to the back and with a small pair of sharp scissors cut through the bobbin thread of the satin-stitching. Turn your work to the right side, pull the top thread above where you have cut and it should unravel like magic.

Free-machine stitching/ Embroidery

FREE-MACHINE STITCHING

Free-machine stitching can be used for embellishing appliqués, stitching highlights and as an alternative method for attaching some appliqués. It is also the same stitch that is used for machine quilting. Providing you have a stabiliser on the back of your work, you should not need to use a hoop.

To do free-machine stitching you will need a darning foot and you should also be able to lower the feed-dogs or cover them with a plate. However, if this is not possible on your machine (or if fitting the plate does not leave enough room for quilting layers of fabric), then cover the feed-dogs with masking tape. The machine needle will punch a hole for the stitching.

Set your machine for straight stitching with a stitch width and length at 0. Tension should be normal, although you may have to lower it a little depending on your stitching. Bring the bobbin thread up to the top of your work and hold both threads as you take the first few stitches. After that, you can stitch in any direction. It is best to run the machine fairly fast but this will come with practice.

If you have not used this technique before, it is a good idea to practise on a sample piece before stitching on your project. Prepare some stabiliser-backed fabric, at least A4 size. Practise going forwards, backwards, in circles, writing your name, 'drawing' flower shapes. Cover the whole of your sample piece.

USING AN EMBROIDERY OR DARNING FOOT

Although it is possible to take the normal foot off the machine and embroider without a foot at all, it is much easier and safer to use a darning foot. A darning foot usually has a spring that allows it to move up and down while you sew, although some machines have a different system to allow this. It gives support as the needle makes a stitch but also allows you to move the fabric freely at the same time.

On most Husqvarna-Viking machines, you must select the darning symbol which will release the pressure of the machine foot on the fabric. Some Pfaff machines have a cradle position on the presser lever that lets you free-machine stitch without lowering the presser foot right on to the fabric.

Check with your machine instruction manual or sewing machine dealer, as different makes and models have different adjustments for embroidery. Whichever machine and darning foot you have, it is essential that you lower the presser foot lever before you begin sewing, otherwise you will end up with a terrible tangle of threads on the underside of your work.

MAKING A SAMPLE

It is always a good idea to make a sample or test piece for your project. It should be about A4 size.

Put together pieces of the background fabric and the stabiliser that will be used in the actual project. If you are using the absolute last piece of a special fabric or have not got enough to spare for a sample, then use a substitute fabric of the same weight and type. Fuse some appliqué pieces to it as well. Using this, you can test machine settings, stitches, thread colours and anything else that you have to make a decision about.

Write on the sample what the machine settings or colours and so on are and you have a record of what is right for the project.

This saves much unpicking on the real thing.

The Appliqué Method

DOUBLE-SIDED FUSIBLE WEBBINGS

Many brands and types of fusible webbings can be used for appliqué, ranging through light weight, medium weight to heavy weight. For example, 'Heat N Bond Lite', 'Wonder Under'/'Vliesofix,' 'Steam A Seam', 'Steam A Seam 2', 'Fus A Bond' and 'Appli-kay Wonder' to name some. A couple of these have sticky backs after the appliqué shapes have been cut out and the backing paper removed. This means that you can 'audition' them in position on your background fabric before heat-fixing them with the iron. Read the instructions on the packet before choosing the one that is most suitable for your project.

Because I often work with fine cottons, silks or sometimes synthetics, I choose to use Vliesofix/Wonder Under. This product has very fine glue bubbles on the back of it which means that you never see any of the glue spots showing through on the right side of fine fabrics.

For ease and consistency I will refer to Vliesofix throughout the text but any of the other products may be substituted.

Vliesofix is double-sided fusible webbing with tracing paper on one side. It makes appliqué very simple, provided you remember one thing — your design must be drawn *in reverse* on the Vliesofix.

To reverse the image, hold or tape the design face down on to a light box or a window with the light shining through it. You will then be able to trace your designs from the reverse side of the paper very easily.

Sometimes you will need the flower and leaf designs facing both ways. Trace the flower and leaf designs from the book on to firm tracing paper so that you will be able to use both sides. Trace all the pieces to be cut from the one fabric in a block and handle them as one at this stage.

There is no need to consider the grain-line of the fabric when placing the traced design pieces. You can take advantage of patterned fabric or just place pieces for the least wasteful use of the fabric.

Cut out the traced motifs, leaving a small margin all around.

Using a medium-heat dry iron, press the rough side of the Vliesofix on to the back of the appliqué fabric. Remember, if you are using synthetic or delicate fabrics protect them from the direct heat of the iron with an appliqué mat or silicone paper (baking paper). Cut out the traced shapes exactly from the fabric.

Decide where you will place them on the background fabric. Peel off the backing paper from the Vliesofix on each of the appliqués. Making sure that each piece is situated correctly, use a medium-heat dry iron and press the pieces into position on the background.

USING VLIESOFIX

Step 1.
Design (with the underlaps marked).

Step 2.
Draw pieces separately in reverse.

Step 3.
Iron on to the reverse side
of the fabric.

Step 4.
Cut out.

Step 5.
Assemble the pieces on the background and fuse in place.

Japanese Flowers in Appliqué

Step 6.
Fuse iron-on tearaway to the back. Satin stitch the edges and free-machine the details.

Stabilisers

IRON-ON TEARAWAY STABILISER

What you need for successful appliqué is an iron-on stabiliser that can be torn away after you have finished stitching. Before beginning any machine stitching, your work should be backed with an iron-on stabiliser. It should extend at least 2.5 cm (1 in) beyond all the appliqué pieces. This will give a firm base on which to appliqué and free-machine stitch. The stabiliser is torn away after the stitching has been completed. If the work is not stabilised, the stitching will pull it out of shape and it will never sit flat.

One such stabiliser is Vilene's 'Stitch and Tear Fusible' or 'Iron-on Tearaway' (BU8030). It looks and feels like waxed lunch wrap. The smooth side is ironed to the back of your background fabric.

There are a number of different stabilisers, but many are for use in a hoop with automatic embroidery machines and they are not the iron-on variety. These will not hold your work firmly enough for appliqué.

It helps to tack the stabiliser around the edges as it can have an annoying tendency to either peel off or get caught under the presser foot as you are stitching. Stitch the pieces in place and complete any free-machine embroidery.

Take care when you tear the stabiliser away from any embroidery. Hold the embroidery stitching with one finger while you carefully tear around it.

Some stabilisers adhere to the fabric more firmly than others. Be careful not to 'burn' any stabiliser on; it is very difficult to remove. Use just sufficient heat to adhere it to the fabric, then tear it away immediately after stitching.

IRON-ON VILENE

This stabiliser does not tear off.

It is used for the three-dimensional butterflies. Medium- to heavyweight iron-on Vilene is best. However, the lightweight one gives a lovely soft finish and you can use two or three layers to give more stiffness. Iron-on Vilene has a grain-line, so if you do use two or more layers, iron the second layer with the grain-line at right angles to the first. For three layers, the third layer will be laid down in the same direction as the first one. This will keep your work flat.

The Butterflies

There are two methods for making the butterflies:

Method 1. Draw your own from the patterns.
Trace butterflies from the given patterns and follow instructions for using Vliesofix
Steps 1 - 4.

*Trace butterfly design onto
Vliesofix, fuse to the back of
the fabric and cut out.*

Method 2. Broderie Perse appliqué.

Instead of drawing your own butterflies, you can make use of butterflies on a printed fabric.

To do this, fuse a piece of Vliesofix to the back of your chosen motif and then cut it out.

Back the fabric with Vliesofix and cut out the chosen butterflies.

MAKING THE BUTTERFLIES THREE-DIMENSIONAL

1. Cut a piece of backing fabric large enough to hold all the 3D butterflies, plus 1 cm ($^3/_8$ in) all round. Choose an appropriate colour for the backing fabric if it is likely to show.

2. Depending on how firm you want the butterflies, cut either one or two pieces of iron-on Vilene the same size as the backing fabric and fuse it (or them) to the backing fabric. Consider using black or grey Vilene if your fabrics are dark in colour.

3. Peel the tracing paper from the Vliesofix on the butterflies and arrange them on top of the Vilene. Fuse them into place and satin-stitch or free-machine around them. If you satin-stitch with gold thread, use a similar yellow colour polyester thread in the bobbin. If they are free-machined, then stitch around the shapes twice. Some free-machine or hand embroidery can also be done at this stage.

4. Cut out the appliqués. It is easiest to use a small pair of sharp scissors and angle them underneath the work, taking care not to cut the satin-stitching threads. Leaving the tiniest possible margin of backing will help, and these tiny pieces will fall or pull away afterwards. If you do cut a thread — as nearly always happens — use Fray-Stop or clear craft glue on the end of a toothpick to prevent the stitches unravelling.

5. The cut edges of the Vilene can be coloured with a fabric marker pen that matches the edge thread colour. Double-ended textile markers are available in several brands (for example, Fabrico) in a range of colours. If the project will not be washed, ordinary felt-tipped markers will do.

Construct a 'sandwich' of backing fabric and iron-on Vilene.
Fuse butterflies to the top layer of Vilene. Satin-stitch the outlines and
free-machine wing details as necessary. Cut out close to the stitching.

Constructing
the Quilt Top

ut the blocks to size but don't forget about the seam allowance. It is best to allow *at least* 1.75 cm (½ in) seams on each one as the appliqué can sometimes distort the fabric. They can then be cut to the correct size after the appliqués are stitched.

Back each block with iron-on tearaway stabiliser.

Following the instructions for 'The Appliqué Method' stitch all the appliqués in place. Refer to the flower patterns and placement diagrams to construct the blocks shown on the quilt. Complete the free-machining details on the flowers and leaves. Reverse the wisteria pattern for the second block.

The iris on the bottom right-hand side of the quilt cannot be appliquéd on until all the blocks and sashings have been put together.

Remove as much stabiliser as possible and press the blocks.

Cut each block to the required size, leaving a 5 mm (¼ in) seam allowance.

Using the border fabric, attach a 1 cm (½ in) wide border to each block and press again. Cut border strips 2 cm (1 in) wide.

Japanese Flowers in Appliqué

BLOCK LAYOUT

IRIS A
34 cm x 21 cm
13½ in x 8¼ in

WATERLILY A
34 cm x 21 cm
13½ in x 8¼ in

ROSE A
14 cm x 21 cm
5½ in x 8¼ in

PEONY A
21 cm x 33 cm
8¼ in x 13¼ in

CHRYSANTHEMUM A
21 cm x 34 cm
8¼ in x 13½ in

IRIS B
9 cm x 22 cm
3½ in x 8¾ in

IRIS C
18 cm x 22 cm
7¼ in x 8¾ in

IRIS D
9 cm x 22 cm
3½ in x 8¾ in

CAMELLIA A
17 cm x 34 cm
6½ in x 13½ in

WISTERIA A
8.5 cm x 22 cm
3¼ in x 8½ in

WISTERIA B
8.5 cm x 22 cm
3¼ in x 8½ in

ROSE B
20 cm x 12 cm
8 in x 4¾ in

PEONY B
20 cm x 32 cm
8 in x 12½ in

HYDRANGEA A
21 cm x 14 cm
8¼ in x 5½ in

WATERLILY B
42 cm x 21 cm
16½ in x 8¼ in

CHRYSANTHEMUM B
20 cm x 31 cm
8 in x 11¾ in

CAMELLIA B
21 cm x 34 cm
8¼ in x 13½ in

HYDRANGEA B
20 cm x 11 cm
8 in x 4 in

IRIS E
42 cm x 21 cm
16½ in x 8¼ in

BLOSSOMS
44 cm x 13 cm
17¾ in x 5½ in

Refer to 1. on page 60

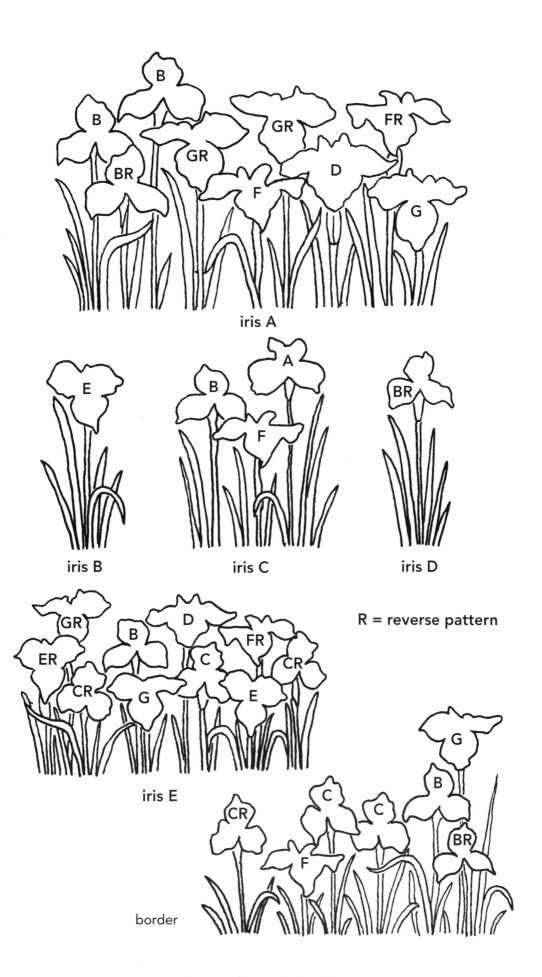

iris A

iris B

iris C

iris D

R = reverse pattern

iris E

border

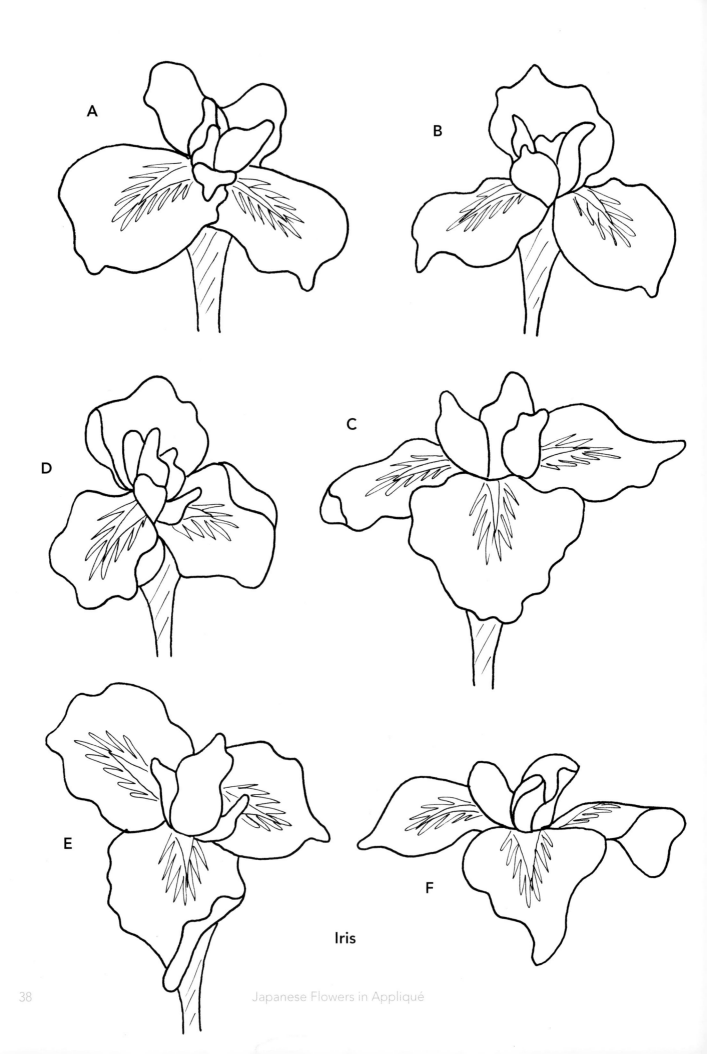

A

B

C

D

E

F

Iris

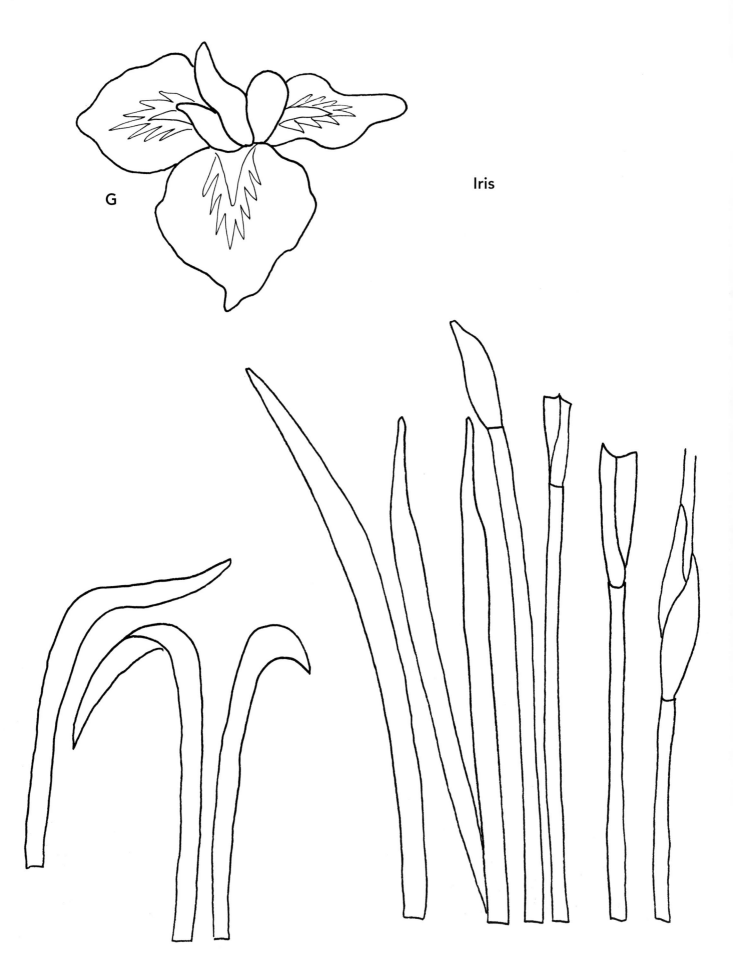

G

Iris

PEONY: BLOCKS A AND B

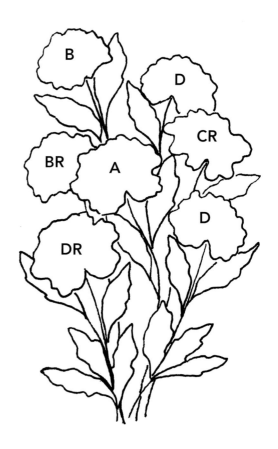

Peony A

R = reverse pattern

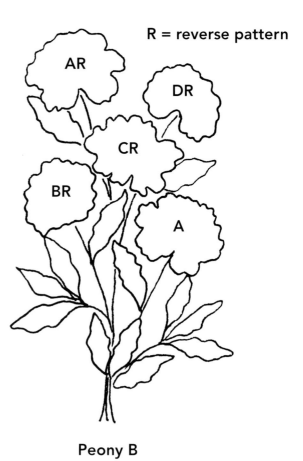

Peony B

Japanese Flowers in Appliqué

Peony

A

B

C

D

Chrysanthemum A

Chrysanthemum B

R = reverse pattern

Chrysanthemum

A

Aa

B

C

D

E

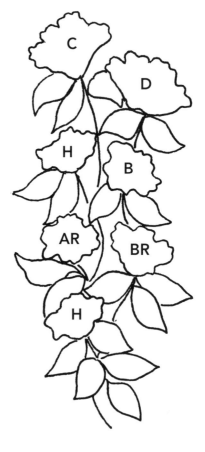

Camellia A

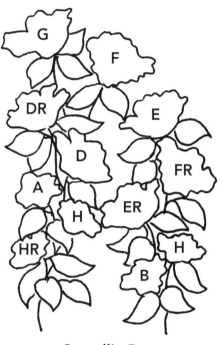

Camellia B

R = reverse pattern

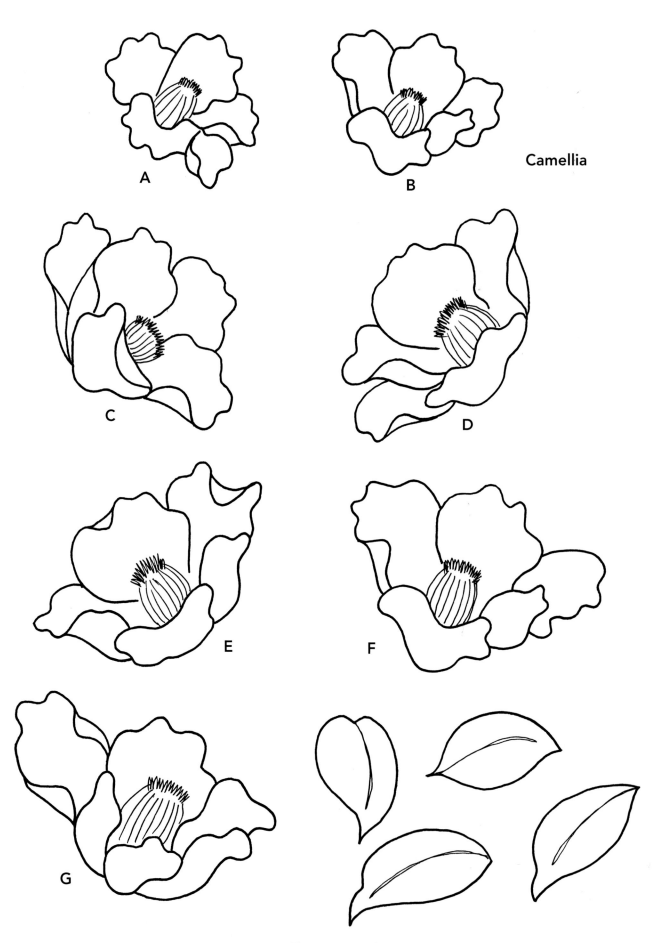

Camellia

A

B

C

D

E

F

G

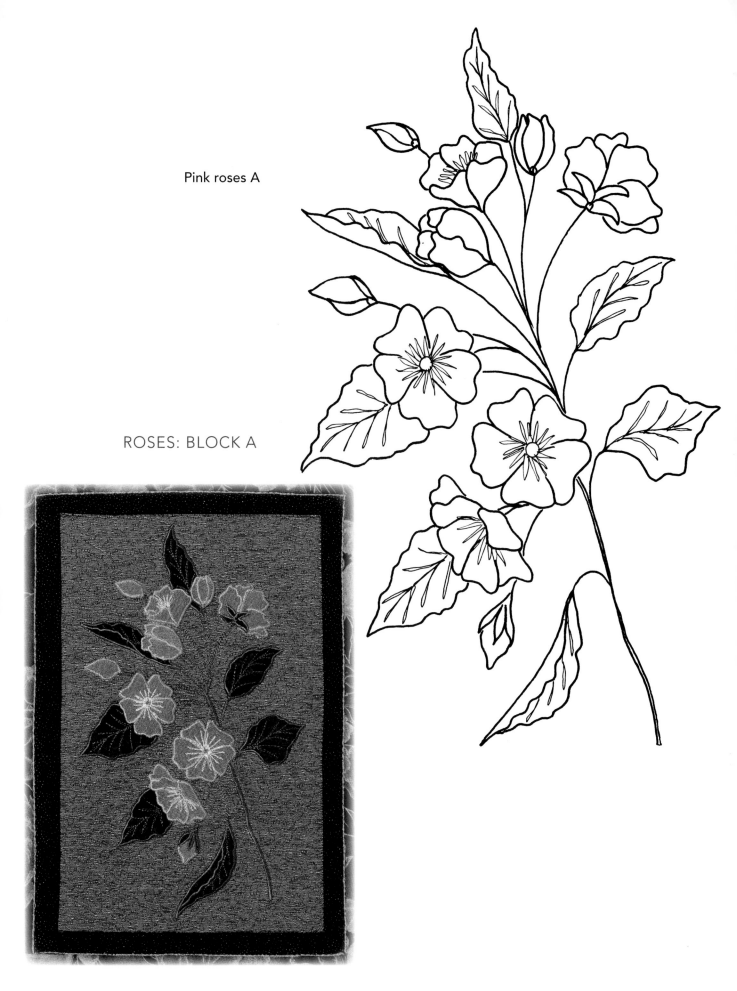

Pink roses A

ROSES: BLOCK A

White roses B

**Wisteria
A & B (reverse)**

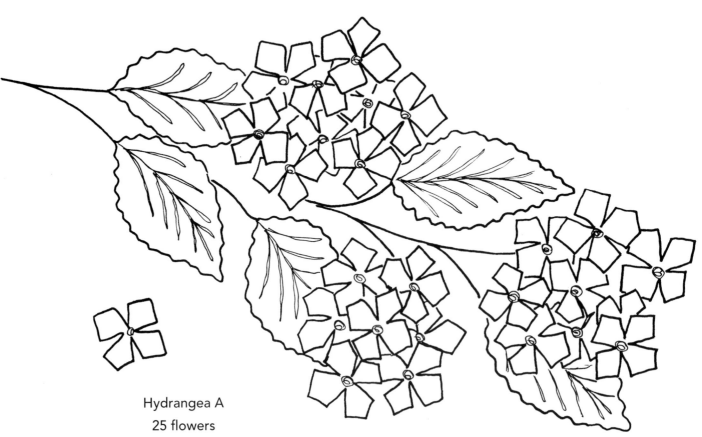

Hydrangea A
25 flowers

Japanese Flowers in Appliqué

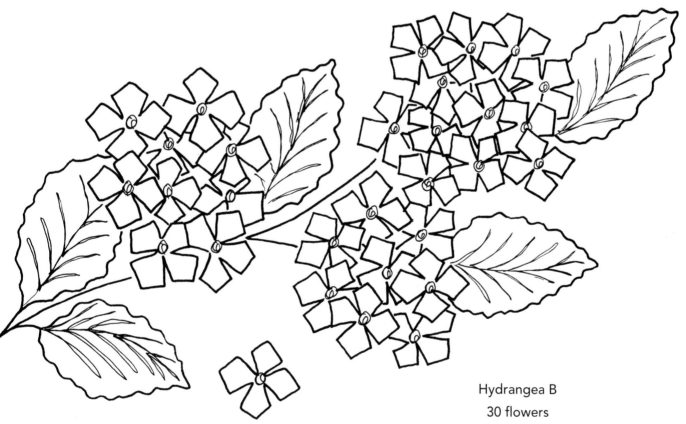

Hydrangea B
30 flowers

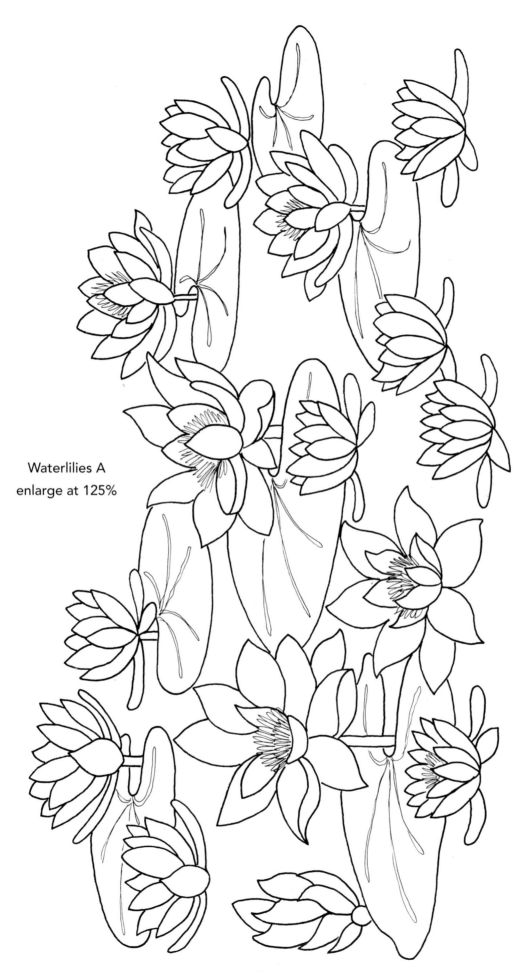

Waterlilies A
enlarge at 125%

Waterlilies B
enlarge at 125%

BLOSSOM

Japanese Flowers in Appliqué

Blossom
enlarge at 165%

JOINING THE BLOCKS TOGETHER

1. The bottom right-hand iris block has an extra 3.5 cm (1¼ in) wide sashing and 1 cm (½ in) wide border to the bottom of it. Attach these two pieces first. Add a seam allowance of 1 cm (½ in) to each.

2. Follow the layout diagram and piece the blocks together with 2 cm (¾ in) wide sashing. Cut all sashing 3 cm (1¼ in) wide to include seam allowance.

3. Add a 2 cm (¾ in) sashing around the completed blocks. Cut sashing 3 cm (1¼ in) wide to include seam allowance.

4. Add a 10 cm (4 in) border. Cut border 11 cm (4 ½ in) wide to include seam allowance.

5. Lastly, another 2 cm (¾ in) sashing. Cut sashing 3 cm (1¼ in) wide to include seam allowance.

THE LAST GROUP OF IRIS

Fuse the last group of iris in place. The bottom of the stems should go right to the edge of the sashing.

Fuse iron-on stabiliser on the back of your work to cover this last group of iris flowers.

Complete the satin-stitching and free-machine embroidery.

Tear the stabiliser away.

Putting the Quilt Together

For machine quilting, prepare your backing, which should be 5 cm (2 in) bigger all round than the quilt top. Lay it out wrong side up on a smooth flat surface, such as a large table or the floor. Pull the edges of the backing taut, but do not stretch them, and tape down the corners and the centres of the sides with masking tape. Use a couple more pieces of tape on each side for a large piece. Place the batting, which should be the same size as the backing, on the backing and smooth it out. If you have to join pieces of batting, butt the edges together and sew them with a diagonal basting stitch. Do not overlap them or you will have a ridge in the finished quilt. (A hairdryer helps to remove fold marks and fluff up the batting.) Tape the batting into position, then place your thoroughly pressed quilt top, right side up, on top of the batting, making sure that the centres of the quilt top edges line up with the centre points on the edges of the backing. Tape the quilt top in place.

SAFETY PINS

Beginning at the centre of one edge and working to one corner, then working from the centre edge again to the other corner, put in 2.5 cm (1 in) safety pins, about 5 cm (2 in) apart. Move to the opposite side of the quilt and repeat, and then do the last two sides. You will now have safety pins right round the edge of the quilt. Use the back of a spoon or a round-tipped pâté knife to lift the pin as you close it. It is much faster and it saves your fingers!

Working from the edges toward the centre of the quilt, place safety pins 8-10 cm (3-4 in) apart over the entire quilt. You will need about 400-500 pins. Try not to place pins where you intend to stitch — for example, in-the-ditch or on any sashing. Avoid pinning appliqués; if at all possible pin around them. Be very careful when pinning silk as it marks so easily. Pin against appliqués or in a spot that will be covered by quilting.

Remove the tape and you are ready for quilting. When you remove the pins during quilting make sure that you open them right out as you lift them free. This is very important, especially when the pins are in silk fabric as it stops any threads from being pulled. Pinning in this manner and taking out the pins as you go is much easier than pulling basting threads out from under machine quilting.

Japanese Flowers in Appliqué

Quilting

Attach the walking foot to the machine.

Use polyester thread to match the backing in the bobbin and either monofilament thread or a thread to blend with the quilt fabrics on the top.

Roll half the quilt and put it under the arm of the machine so that you can begin quilting in the centre of the quilt.

Begin quilting in-the-ditch, working from the centre out to the edge of the quilt. Pull the bobbin thread through to the top and start and stop each section of quilting with some stitches very close together.

Re-roll the quilt and complete the opposite side.

Turn the quilt and repeat the process for the last two quarters.

Attach the darning foot and outline all the flowers. Use monofilament thread to stipple quilt around the flowers.

QUILTING THE LEAVES IN THE BORDER

The pattern for a corner group is given. Use combinations of the other groups to fit the rest of the border.

Use an H or HB pencil to trace groups of leaves on to paper such as Stitch n' Tear or greaseproof paper. Do not use a very soft lead pencil as the lead tends to mark the quilt as it is stitched. Leave a margin of at least 4 cm (1½ in) all round. Use at least four straight pins, one per corner, to pin it to the area to be quilted.

Use gold thread and free-machine stitch over the tracings.

Because of the complex design, you must backtrack over some parts to keep the stitching flowing. To stitch the veins in the centres of the leaves, begin in the centre and stitch in and out over the same lines.

When you have finished, tear the paper away. Tweezers are very useful for removing the last small scraps of paper.

When all the leaves have been quilted, stipple quilt around them.

The leaves have been traced on to paper and stitched. Half the paper has been torn away.
Heavy gold thread has been couched in-the-ditch using a braiding foot.

Corner quilting design

enlarge at 112%

Groups of leaves
for border

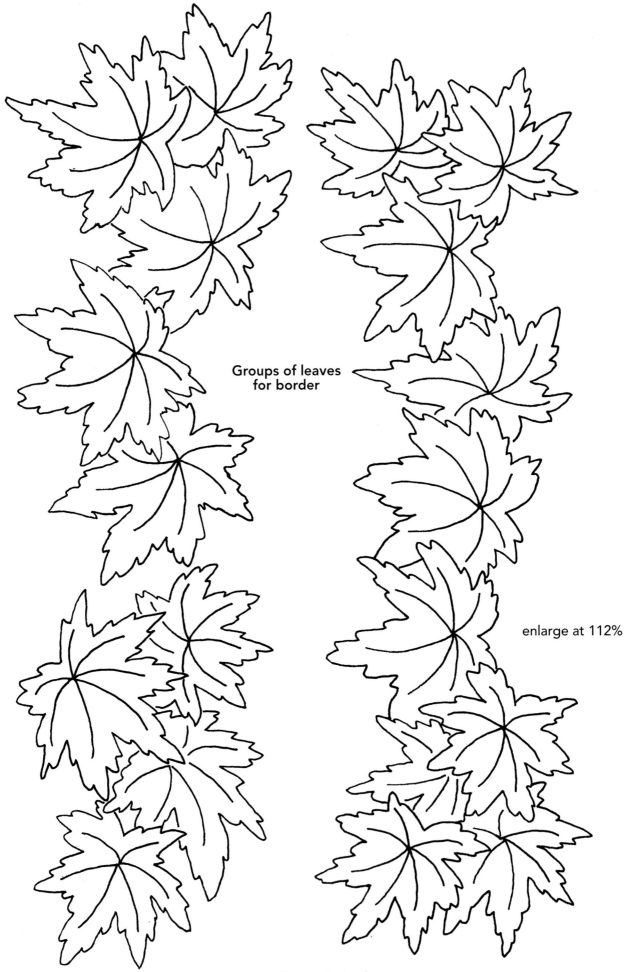

Groups of leaves
for border

enlarge at 112%

COUCHING THE GOLD THREAD

Heavy gold thread outlines all the sashing. It is too thick to go through the machine so it must be couched down. Using a braiding foot will allow you to guide the thread easily in-the-ditch. With monofilament thread through the needle and a polyester thread in the bobbin to match the backing fabric, use a zigzag stitch about 1.5 mm (less than $^1/_{16}$ in) long and 1.5 mm (less than $^1/_{16}$ in) wide.

To begin, use a tapestry needle to insert the thread into the batting layer. Push the needle through the quilt top and into the batting layer without catching the backing. Bring the needle out about 2.5 cm (1 in) from where you will begin stitching. Leave a short tail of thread hanging out. To finish, thread the tapestry needle, insert the needle at the end of the last stitch and bring it out about 2.5 cm (1 in) away from the stitching. Cut the tails level with the top of the quilt and they will pull into the batting out of sight.

THE BINDING

Trim the backing and batting so that you will have 1.5 cm (½ in) to enclose in the binding.

Attach a 4 cm (1½ in) strip of binding to quilt top (right sides together) mitring the corners. Turn the binding strip over and slip stitch in place on the back.

ATTACHING THE THREE-DIMENSIONAL BUTTERFLIES

The butterflies are the last addition to be attached to the quilt.

Begin by fusing the Vliesofixed body to the wings and satin-stitching or free-machining it to the quilt.

Use monofilament thread and free-machine the line marked A. Push the wing tips B and C down slightly and free-machine from the body to the wing tip. Push D and E slightly upwards and stitch the bottom wing in place. The outer edges of the wings are left free.

The feelers can then be free-machined directly onto the quilt.

Attach a label with the quilt title, your name and the date to the back of the quilt and you are finished.

Glossary

Appliqué

Stitching fabric shapes to a background to create a design or a picture.

Braiding foot

A machine foot that is used for guiding a heavy thread that is being couched down by machine.

Broderie Perse

This is a term used for cutting out the printed design on one fabric and stitching it onto another fabric.

Cornelli (see stipple quilting)

Couching

Couching is the term used for laying down a thick thread that will not go through the machine needle by stitching over it with a fine thread. The heavy thread can be guided in position using a braiding foot.

Darning foot

This can also be called an *embroidery foot*. It is a machine foot that can be used for free-machining or darning. It often, but not always, has a spring mechanism. The feed-dogs are lowered so that stitching is possible in any direction. (See using an embroidery or darning foot page 18.)

Feed-dogs or feed-teeth

These are the 'teeth' under the top plate of the machine that feed the fabric through the machine as you stitch.

Free-machine stitching

When the feed-dogs are lowered and a darning foot is attached to the machine it enables you to stitch in any direction. Some machines have a plate to cover the feed-dogs instead of lowering them. Free-machining is also called free-motion work. It is the same technique that is used for free-machine quilting.

In-the-ditch

Seams are generally pressed to one side rather than pressed open for quilting projects. Quilting in-the-ditch is stitching right in the seam line on the low side of the seam.

Silicone paper

Baking paper, the sort you use for lining cake tins.

Stabilisers

Iron-on tearaway

This is a temporary iron-on stabiliser that holds the work firm for satin-stitching and free-machine embroidery. After the stitching is complete it is torn away. Satin stitching and free-machining need this type of stabiliser so that the work does not stretch out of shape as it is stitched.

Iron-on Vilene

An iron-on stabiliser that is meant to stay in place, not to be torn away. It is used for making the three-dimensional butterflies for this quilt.

Stipple quilting

This is a free-machining stitch sometimes called meandering or cornelli stitch (like cake icing) that resembles a fine 'scribble' pattern to fill in a background. The line of stitching meanders around the appliqués without crossing over itself.

Vliesofix

A double-sided fusible webbing with tracing paper on one side. Vliesofix is one brand but there are many others. (See 'The Applique Method' page 19.)

Walking foot

A machine foot that has 'teeth' that work in conjunction the feed-dogs. It is an excellent foot for straight line quilting as the three layers of the quilt are fed evenly through the machine.

About the Author

Eileen Campbell worked as a primary school teacher for a total of 22 years. She has an interest and expertise in many crafts, including weaving and related textile arts, fabric printing, bookbinding, calligraphy and photography. She began patchwork and quilting in 1984, and since 1993 has been working as a textile artist, giving workshops and lectures both in Australia and overseas.

Eileen has written three books, 'Appliqué Applied' (1994), 'U is for Unicorn', which has since been re-titled as 'Creative Medieval Designs for Appliqué' (1998) and 'Ideas for Appliqué' (2008) all published by Sally Milner Publishing Pty Ltd. She also designs patterns for sale.

Her quilts have won many awards in Australia and abroad. They have been included in The Husqvarna Viking International Challenge 'Feel Free' and also in their 'Color, Couleur, Colore, Kulor' International Challenge.

Her quilt, 'Pelican Twilight', won 'Best of World' in the 'World Quilt and Textile Competition' (USA) 2002.

'Iris Variations' won 'Best Machine Workmanship' Innovative section in the 'World Quilt and Textile Contest' (USA) 2007.

She was an invited artist for the Japanese travelling exhibition *Contemporary Images in Japanese Quilts* 2004, and was a contributor to the 'Three Countries Challenge' (Japan, Australia and France) 2006.

Eileen specialises in machine work using appliqué, embroidery and quilting techniques. Her designs usually incorporate flora and fauna whether from nature or imagination and are often embellished with beads, braids etc. and machine quilted.